Mastering Memory

LINDA FULKERSON

Copyright © 2015 Linda Fulkerson
All rights reserved.

DISCLAIMER

Please note the information is presented "as is" with no guarantees of success. Results may vary depending upon a person's preexisting health conditions and the amount of effort put into the tactics and principles explained in this eBook.

CONTENTS

	Introduction	1
1	Memory and Memory Problems	5
2	Using Mnemonic Devices	11
3	The Mindful Approach	17
4	Mind Tricks	27
5	Your Lifestyle	33
6	Mastering Memory	47
7	Bonus: Checklist	55
	About the Author	58

Introduction

What this eBook Can Teach You

Have you ever been embarrassed due to a poor memory? I know I have. I struggled to recall important information, muddled details of conversations, and not only faltered to remember the names of new acquaintances, but often had forgotten I already met people. I reached the point where I was continually apologizing for my poor memory. My forgetfulness wasn't just embarrassing, it cost me time, money, and increased my stress level. I was totally frustrated with my inability to remember things.

The good news is, I discovered memory skills can be improved. Plus, many things that can be controlled affect memory, so I did some research and compiled my findings into this short eBook in hopes of helping others who are plagued by poor memory. Here's what I learned — by making some adjustments in my lifestyle, practicing a few memory-enhancement techniques, and becoming more mindful, those who suffer from poor memory can finally set their minds at ease. Literally. Which is great news for those of us who are middle-age and beyond, because statistics prove memory naturally declines as we age.

In fact, the hippocampus part of our brain — where our brain builds memory — loses 5 percent of its nerve cells every decade we're alive. Yikes! Plus, aging prohibits the production of the neurotransmitter, acetylcholine — which is necessary to both memory and the learning process. But, studies show with a little effort, the brain's aging process can actually be slowed, which is great news!

The information you'll learn in this eBook will help you stave off age-related memory loss and boost your memory power significantly. This eBook will help you see how important your memory is to staying young and vital. Studies have proven that those who exercise their brains can actually ward off early symptoms of Alzheimer's disease and dementia.

Here's an overview of what you'll learn in this eBook:

Chapter One: Memory and Memory Problems

This chapter explains what memory is and gives an overview of some memory disorders.

Chapter Two: Using Mnemonic Devices

In this chapter, you'll be introduced to the simple ways you can assimilate volumes of information into your brain in order to have quick and easy access. The mnemonic devices you'll learn about include association, visualization, and observation.

Chapter Three: The Mindful Approach

Using the Mindful Approach can help you perfect your memory skills by using some mindful memory techniques. The military has used such techniques to reduce Post Traumatic Stress Disorder (PTSD) in troops who have returned home after being deployed in a battle zone.

Chapter Four: Memory Tricks

Here you'll learn how to trick your brain into remembering. Simple tricks, such as moving your eyes, chewing gum, deep breathing, and more are discussed in this chapter.

Chapter Five: Your Lifestyle

The information shared in this chapter was especially helpful to me. Lifestyle has everything to do with how our memory (and our body) ages. Both brain and body must be fed and exercised properly to get the nutrition they need to function and to withstand the affects of aging. This chapter will suggest some lifestyle and habit changes that can lead you in a direction to enhance your memory rather than harm it.

Chapter Six: Mastering Your Memory — One Step at a Time

This chapter wraps up the main section of this book, and will send you on your way with the tools you need to withstand the ravages of time and preserve your memory well into your later years.

You'll learn how to control your mind so you know you're doing everything you can to keep your mind as active as possible. This eBook can help you relax about little things, such as forgetting where you put your keys, and help equip you to keep your memory intact. Plus, in this chapter, you'll find action item guides you can refer to as needed.

Bonus Material: Mastering Memory Checklist

This handy checklist can be used as a quick reference guide of the material you learned in this eBook.

CHAPTER ONE
Memory and Memory Problems

Just what is memory?

Many people use the word "memory" without fully understanding what it is or how it works. Your memory is a complex system that can dictate your day-to-day behavior. Here are several definitions of memory:
1. A process of how your brain stores and remembers information
2. Something that is remembered from your past
3. The remembering of a deceased person, as "in memory of"
4. The length of time a person or event is remembered
5. The part of a computer where data is stored and retrieved

The Three Stages of Memory

To get a big more technical, your memory has three stages: encoding, storage, and retrieval.
- The **encoding** process is the first stage, and this is where you absorb information.
- The **storage** process is where your memory creates a permanent record of the information.
- The **retrieval** process is the act of you remembering or retrieving the stored information.

One common complaint most people find is that they start to forget things, especially as they get older. This is known as forgetfulness or amnesia.

When it comes to the actual process of remembering you go through three stages: **sensory memory**, **short-term memory**, and **long-term** memory.

Your sensory memory identifies and holds information for just a few seconds. When you look at something for just a second and can still remember details, this is your sensory memory in action.

Your short-term memory allows you to recall items for anywhere from a few seconds up to one minute without rehearsing. Most people can remember chunks of information that have approximately 4 to 5 components, or "chunks."

An example of this is the way in which most people learn to remember a phone number. You simply break it into chunks that include the area code, then the next 3 numbers and then the final numbers.

Your long-term memory is capable of storing information for long periods of time. This time limit is almost unlimited. Those phone numbers that you remember may be first stored in your short-term memory, but because you can remember them for years, this indicates that they are stored in your long-term memory.

Information that is repeated ends up in your long-term memory, allowing you to retrieve it automatically.

Help for Short-Term Memory Lapses

Your short-term memory is connected to the memories and information you are currently aware of. These memories only last seconds and most people can store four pieces of information during this time. The term short-term memory can be viewed as a temporary storage stage.

What happens to many people is they often experience memory lapses. These are directly associated with your short-term memory.

You have probably experienced this yourself. Have you ever walked into your kitchen and then forgot why you went there? Or you start to say something and forget what you were talking about. I've done that a lot!

Dealing with a memory lapse is very common for anyone who is dealing with a lot of stress and in those who have a lack of focus. These short lapses are common and are nothing to worry about, if they happen occasionally.

There are several things you can do to improve your short-term memory. Writing things down can help you remember important information. Use the note app on your smart phone to jot things down. Or you may want to use a notebook on your desk. Using sticky notes and placing them in strategic places is another great tactic to use.

Make use of the calendars and to-do lists on your mobile and home devices. These can often be synched together so your list is always current.

Word and picture association games work extremely well. Sometimes all you need do is to repeat someone's name out loud when you first meet them. This helps you create a mental image of the person and your memory associates this with the name.

Do you forget where you put things? You can't remember where you left your car keys or your phone? Make a point of creating a place for these items. You could hang keys on a hook and place your phone near the door so you can grab both on the way out.

Many people can benefit from developing a system or routine. This could be done by setting Saturdays as laundry day or Wednesdays as grocery shopping after work day.

Mentally repeating your list of things to do each day can help with your short-term memory. Tell yourself you need your car keys or phone. Use the word 'I' to solidify the action into your brain. I've also learned to say, "I'm putting my car keys here," when I set them down.

Many times people may think they have a memory problem when all they are is not decisive enough. Maybe your subconscious is putting something off because it is too hard to do. Or it may be a task that you find unpleasant or overwhelming. It may not be that you're actually forgetting to do a certain task, but that you're mentally balking (procrastinating) about doing it.

If this sounds like you, then try breaking larger tasks into much smaller ones. If your garage or basement needs cleaning out, do it in steps, over a period of weekends, instead of trying to do it in one day. This way you will feel good that you made a start and accomplished something.

Not All Memory Problems Are Equal

Many people suffer from a condition known as memory weakness. While this is present in adults, many children have this condition, too, and it can be connected to several learning disabilities.

If you find your child doesn't always seem to be paying attention, or they say they never said something you are certain they did, these can all be signs of having a memory weakness.

The medical term for this is Auditory Reversal. This occurs when a person's long-term auditory retrieval is stronger than their long term storage ability.

This long-term retrieval process works in a way similar to a magnet. The memory can only pull out as much information as the magnet will allow. When the pull is greater than the storage, additional and unrelated information is pulled out. This extra information will not be part of the actual conversation and is how you may think someone is not paying attention to you.

While this new information is not part of the conversation it is often related in a small way. To the person or child it is related. Let's look at an example of this.

You allowed your daughter to go to her friend's house and said that she could stay for dinner, but then she was to come straight home. With auditory reversal she may think that you told her she could stay and watch a movie after dinner. She comes home late and is in trouble because she didn't listen to you and do what she was told.

Not many people are aware of this condition, and when told by their family doctor, feel bad about disciplining their child for the wrong thing. The child is not disobeying, their brain literally gave them the wrong information. It can help to talk more slowly and to look them directly in the eye when giving them instructions.

One common side effect of living with a weak memory is that children or teenagers develop disrespect for rules and authority. All they see is the adult figures in their life keep on changing the rules to suit their own purpose. This is one reason why many children and teens seem to be so rebellious and frustrated.

Once this memory weakness or Auditory Retrieval is identified, it can be dealt with. The process required is one that helps the child improve their memory skills and will eventually help balance out the push and pull effect. If you suspect your child may have memory weakness, consult with a health care professional to have their condition assessed.

But most memory issues aren't due to such a condition. Most of us who struggle with poor memory are just plain forgetful. And the content of this eBook can help you overcome that!

Nobody's Memory Is Perfect

Do you feel as though your memory is pathetic? You tend to forget what you are doing and can't recall the simplest of things? That's where I was! And people who struggle with imperfect memory are not alone. Hundreds of people, if not more, feel as though their memories are not working the way they should. Many people spend a lot of money on counselors and equipment to help boost their memory, but most of the time, memory can be bolstered by using a few memory tricks and implementing some lifestyle changes.

You may be surprised to know that noone has a perfect memory. Your memory is a very complex thing, and it can be difficult to understand how it really works.

One thing to keep in mind with your memory is that certain events can cause you to remember or not remember them. For example, if you were a witness to a traumatic event, you may remember the event in different ways.

Firstly, you may not remember it at all. Your brain has the ability to block out unpleasant things when it wants too. This is known as a coping mechanism and helps your brain deal with what you had witnessed.

On the other hand, you may find you can't stop seeing the traumatic event in your mind. You remember things in such fine detail, you may even think you are going crazy.

Your lifestyle can affect your memory and the way it functions. Certain things such as eating a healthy diet and exercising regularly can help you maintain good memory function.

Exercise is thought to release proteins in your brain which help improve your memory. Many older people who reported having a bad memory started exercising regularly. After exercising for just a short time period, they found their memory improved.

Sleep is another important factor when it comes to your memory. As you are aware, your body requires sleep and plenty of it. When you become sleep-deprived, your memory and your entire body suffers.

Basically, when you sleep your memory opens up new pathways. In a person who gets enough sleep, these pathways are working at an optimal performance level. This allows them to learn a new task more efficiently than a person who is tired.

In addition to a healthy diet, proper rest, and exercise, you actually need to use and challenge your memory. If you don't read very often or do any types of puzzles, your brain gets lazy. You need to use your brain and memory on a regular basis.

There are lots of options you can use to challenge your memory and get it working again, the way it should. Many of those will be covered in this eBook. So, your memory may not pathetic, it may just need a challenge.

CHAPTER TWO

Using Mnemonic Devices

What are mnemonic devices?

The word "mnemonics" comes from the Greek Goddess of memory — Mnemosyne, and the term broadly refers to a group of memory techniques to help people quickly and easily assimilate volumes of information for easy access.

One of the best ways to increase your memory power is to use Mnemonic devices such as association, rhymes, and acronyms. When you learn how to use these methods effectively, you'll be "encoding" the memories in your brain and will be better able to recall specific information.

Everything is faster and more accurately recalled by using Mnemonics, including faces, figures, events, and names. It's also much more fun than the ordinary method of repetition to remember and recall because Mnemonics uses the senses (sound, touch, sight and smell).

Mnemonics uses the methods that our brain uses to store information in the following ways:

- **Visualization** — Visualized memories are stronger than text you may read. Most images are alive and vibrant and easy to remember.
- **Observation** — Observing something is different than merely seeing it with your eyes. We pass people in the street that we "see," but don't necessarily commit to memory by observing.
- **Association** — We associate memories without even realizing it. For example, if you meet someone on a plane,

you'll always associate that person with the plane ride experience.

Mnemonics are useful techniques that can help you commit information to your long term memory so you don't have to spend so much time in repetitious memorization.

It's important that you regularly exercise your brain to keep the neural pathways open and your memory sharp. The neural pathways are the parts of your brain that help you recall information, solve problems, and perform tasks you've experienced in the past.

When you exercise your brain, you're stimulating the pathways so they'll stay vital and active. To accomplish the exercises your brain needs, you need to change your routine once in a while and learn and develop new skills.

Types of Mnemonics

You may be more adept at one type of Mnemonics than another, or you may use them all according to what you're attempting to remember. Here are a variety of Mnemonic methods you might want to try:

- **Association** — This is a good method to remember facts and especially helpful if you're a student or have a career where it's imperative that you have instant recall on volumes of factual information. For example, if you need to remember that Franklin Roosevelt was president during World War II, you could associate his last name with an image of roses (for Roose) and velvet (velt). Velvet roses are a good image for the name. To remember numbers, break them down into smaller groupings. For example, if you have trouble remembering your driver's license number and the number is 186543807, you can break it down to 186-438-07. Then, use visualization such as "186" (miles to the next town), "438" (your best friend's phone prefix) and "07" (your condo number). Create your own unique associations for things you need to remember.
- **Rhymes** — Rhymes you've known since your childhood can be perfect mnemonic devices to help you recall

information. The most common one for students might be, "Columbus sailed the ocean blue in fourteen-hundred ninety-two. Students and those who need to remember factual information use associative rhymes all the time to remember. If you can't remember how to spell Mississippi, think "M-I-crooked letter-crooked letter-I-humpback, humpback-I. It's fun, and it works.

- **Chunking** — Another popular method of mnemonics is chunking, which involves grouping things together to form something easy to remember. For example, if you need to remember lettuce, olives, detergent, and envelopes when you're at the supermarket, simply keep the word "L-O-D-E" embedded in your mind. We remember phone numbers more easily because there are spaces between groupings of numbers, but you can do the same for a driver's license number, bank account number, or any other long series of numbers you must know.
- **Acronyms** — Acronyms are mnemonic device great for remembering a large amount of information. You can use acronyms which are already in place (such as H-O-M-E-S, for remember the Great Lakes — Huron, Ontario, Michigan, Erie, and Superior) — or make them up. Ingredients in a recipe can be remembered by making up an acronym such as, B-R-O-C-H for the ingredients: Beans, Rotel, Olives, Chili powder and Hominy, which can be used to make a chili recipe.
- **Acrostics** — Similar to acronyms, acrostics involves creating a sentence out of the first letters of a grouping of words you need to remember. For example, to remember the five elements in the chemistry periodic table (Hydrogen, Helium, Lithium, Beryllium, Boron), you might make up the following sentence: "His Heavy Load Breaks Backs."
- **Loci** — Since ancient Greece, the mnemonic method of Loci has been used to memorize large amounts of information. It involves choosing a path or route you're familiar with and then visualizing and memorizing the things you want to remember along that path. If you have a certain supermarket you like to shop at and are extremely familiar with what items are on the aisles, you probably

arrange your grocery list by aisles and picture going down each one in order of your list.
- **Stacking** — A great memory recall technique that you can use for remember long lists is stacking. To make it work, visualize the items you need to remember in a tall, colorful and "stacked" method. You may want to put yourself on the top of the stack to personalize it. For example, if you need to remember several items at the pet store (treats, food, sweater, leash, and shampoo), you could picture a tall stack of dog food wrapped in a warm doggie sweater with treat bags sticking out of the neck. Put the leash around the neck of the sweater, your dog on top of the stack (with its fur bubbly with shampoo). Easy and fun. Add colors and other "embellishments" to make it more memorable.

All of the above methods are great ways to keep your brain in shape and to ward off such memory problems as dementia and Alzheimer's disease. Keep in mind that the more you work out your brain, the better you'll be able to process and recall information when you need to.

Challenge yourself in different ways. Learn a new skill, language or sport. And, any exercise which requires you to use your hands can also exercise your brain. Take up a musical instrument or some type of needlework to work out the hand-eye coordination area of your brain.

Begin small and simple and then attempt to add information as you're comfortable remembering a half dozen objects or names by using the mnemonic method.

Other Brain Exercises to Stimulate Your Memory

You must exercise your brain just as you would your body for the ultimate fitness and function. Research has proven that regular brain stimulation can keep the brain active and healthy far into later years — a great piece of news for our aging population who are worried about memory loss.

We've mentioned neural pathways. The way the brain works properly is to create new neural pathways which can connect with the stored information. When stimulated, the brain tends to create new pathways to a sort of savings account in the brain, where knowledge is stored and retrieved through the pathways. The more neural pathways, the better retrieval capability.

When people maintain brain function by exercising the brain throughout their lives, a higher level of brain functioning is found. We depend on our brains to remember people's names and faces and even the most minimal things such as where we put our reading glasses.

There are many ways you can keep your brain active and vital well into your later years. Here are a few that you may want to try:

- **Brain tricks** — Some studies show that you can trick your brain into remembering things. Chewing gum while you study is one way — moving your eyes back and forth when trying to memorize is another. We'l learn more about brain tricks in Chapter Three.
- **Focus on one thing at a time** — Unfortunately, multi-tasking has become prevalent in our uber-busy society, but studies show you're much more apt to remember things if you focus on one task at a time.
- **Speak aloud** — When you say aloud what you're attempting to remember something. For example, after you're introduced to a person, repeat his or her name as you're shaking hands. And, like I mentioned earlier, saying out loud where you're putting an item you will need later can help you remember where you put it when you need it.

The brain is a perfect example of the old saying, "If you don't use it, you lose it." Learn something new each day and focus on every task to ensure your brain keeps busy making new pathways and connections for your memory.

Main Points of Chapter Two: Using Mnemonic Devices

When you learn how to use mnemonic devices such as rhyming, association, acrostics, and acronyms, you'll be well on your way to improving your instant recall memory. Below are some important points you should have taken away from this chapter:

- **Association** is a form of mnemonic exercise that involves associating factual information with an image or of breaking up long numbers in a shorter format to remember more easily.
- **Rhymes** can help you recall facts and information. "Columbus sailed in ocean blue in fourteen-hundred ninety-two." Students of all ages find this method easy when trying to memorize volumes of information.
- **Chunking** is also a fun and easy mnemonic device. You'll group things (anything) together to form something that's easy to remember. For example, "Detergent, Olive oil, and Green beans" forms the word, "DOG," which you can then break out into the items when you're at the store.
- **Acronyms** are best for remember a great deal of information for instant recall. Many students recall the Great Lakes for a test by remembering the word, H-O-M-E-S, which translates to Huron, Ontario, Michigan, Erie and Superior.
- **Acrostics** are great ways to remember things that don't make sense otherwise. For example, if you're studying for a health exam in school, make a sentence out of CABS by thinking "Chronic Asthma Brings Sickness." That's just a quick example, but you can create your won acrostics to help you remember things you're studying or for business professionals who have to give a presentation.
- **Loci** has been used since the ancient days of Greece and involves memorizing things or people on a path that you're familiar with. As you walk down the route or path, visualize the things you want to remember appearing along the way.
- **Stacking** is another fun way of using visualization to remember things. You can use your vivid imagination to build a picture of things on a list you must remember.

There are other methods of mnemonics you may want to study, but the above are the top ways to help your memory with the use of mnemonics.

CHAPTER THREE

The Mindful Approach

What is mindfulness?

Mindfulness is a term that gets thrown around a lot at the moment and which is often hailed as some kind of 'solve all' for every kind of problem under the sun. Mindfulness is part self-help technique, part clinical tool and has lately grown to spawn countless eBooks, courses, and evening classes. But what precisely is it and how do you define it?

Mindfulness: An Explanation

Boiled down to its essence, mindfulness is the observation of one's own thoughts and emotions. In other words, it means stepping back and then simply being aware of what you're feeling, what you're thinking and what you are experiencing. This can then in turn be used to help treat a wide range of different psychological problems and to generally improve your psychological health.

The reason for this is that mindfulness brings more attention to the way that we handle various different events and to how our thoughts and emotions normally control us. This then in turn allows us to anticipate them, to deal with them, and ultimately to prevent them.

For instance, someone who deals with social anxiety will likely have a number of ruminations that contribute to their symptoms. These might include worries that they will "make a fool of themselves," that they will be laughed at, that they will stammer . .
.

Many of these thoughts are likely to be inaccurate but it is only by being aware of them that it's possible to manipulate them, to rise above them or to suppress them entirely.

Uses of Mindfulness

When used to combat such conditions as social anxiety, mindfulness can be seen as a clinical tool. Specifically, it is an important part of CBT or Cognitive Behavioral Therapy. This is a psychotherapeutic approach that involves the practice of essentially replacing and reprogramming underlying thoughts, beliefs, and ruminations.

At the same time though, mindfulness has also long been a part of other meditative practices. Here, the goal can often be somewhat different. In the case of enhancing memory, the objective is to be more aware of the present moment in terms of the sensations, the sounds, and the emotions. By practicing this, you can eventually become more 'present' in the moment and better able to react to what's going on around you without judgment and without the constant 'brain chatter' that so many of us experience.

Mindfulness is a broad tool then to be used in a number of different ways. In almost every scenario though, the true end goal is to be aware of the present moment and to find an inner calm that often eludes us.

The Top 10 Benefits of Mindfulness

Mindfulness is a powerful tool that is the perfect tonic to modern day stress and anxiety. But it goes far beyond that and can be instrumental in helping you improve in a vast range of different ways. Read on and we'll go over 10 of these many benefits to demonstrate just how transformative mindfulness really is . . .

1 — It helps reduce stress

Mindfulness teaches us how to be present and how to exist in the moment. This helps us to rise above the stressful thoughts we might be having and even to 'reprogram' them in some cases.

2 — It improves focus

Mindfulness practice requires intense focus and mental discipline. This is something many people are lacking these days owing to the constant distractions we get from our technology and our general ability to get any information or entertainment in seconds. Improving focus can go a long way toward boosting memory function.

3 — It's free and easy

Health organizations love mindfulness because it's something anyone can practice. Once you understand the concept and have been taught the basics, this is something you can do anywhere and with no equipment. It can even be taught over the Internet!

4 — It improves athletic performance

Mindfulness is only one step away from being a 'flow state'. This is a heightened state of awareness and presence that leads to amazing improvements in athletic performance. If you've ever "psyched yourself up" for an event, you likely practiced some form of mindfulness.

5 — It helps sleep

Studies show that mindfulness can be used effectively to combat insomnia.

6 — It can treat panic attacks

Likewise, mindfulness is one of the main treatments used for panic attacks.

7 — It combats negative emotions

In general, mindfulness can be used to make dealing with almost any negative emotion considerably easier.

8 — It enriches life

Being mindful means being present and that in turn means being aware of all the wonderful things happening around you. Instead of being in your own head, you start actually experiencing the world around you. This can even enhance your relationships.

9 — You'll learn about yourself

Learning to observe your own mind is an amazing skill that teaches you about how your own brain works. This is both fascinating and a very useful skill for growth and development.

10 — You'll learn about others

And when you learn more about yourself, you learn more about the minds of others too. Mindfulness will give you the means to help your friends and family and to better manage your relationships with them.

Why Mindfulness is the Perfect Antidote to Modern Living

As much as many of us choose to overlook it, there is a lot wrong with the way most of us currently live our lives. The world we live in changes at such a fast rate, we are continually forced to to adapt and gain abilities and traits that in many ways aren't suitable for us.

We sit in chairs all day long gaining weight, we eat processed foods, and we face constant stresses from work, from our relationships, and from our finances. We're bombarded with a constant flow of information — much of it negative — and that underlying stress affects not only our attitudes and our health in general, but it impacts our memory capabilities.

What's more, we are constantly in demand and constantly plugged in and stressed out. Our phones are always ringing, texts are always coming in, we get a new e-mail every two minutes . . . And even when most of us aren't working or being bothered, we have a near addiction to technology that means we're still unable to really decompress.

Is it any wonder that mental health problems are so rife? I didn't mean to compound the negativity already surrounding most of us, but being aware that stress contributes to memory issues is important to realize as we work to improve our memory. Reducing your stress level can also decrease incidences of forgetfulness.

Using Mindfulness to Escape Modern Stress

This is probably a big part of the reason mindfulness is so popular right now. Mindfulness simply means **directing attention in a purposeful manner**. Sometimes this will mean focusing on our thoughts (in an objective and non-judgmental way), but in other cases it will mean simply being more present and focusing on our breathing and our environment.

Either way, the idea of mindfulness is to enjoy a calmness and to stop the incessant chatter of our minds. When you are completely engaged with the world around you, or when you decide to disengage with your thoughts, it provides you with relief from stress and from fear — and instead allows you to simply relax and recover.

Mindfulness for Concentration

What's more, practicing mindfulness is also the perfect tool for improving concentration, which will in turn, aid with your memory. Mindfulness forces you to develop a mental discipline that is sorely lacking for many of us today. Too often, most of us have 20 things vying for our attention. While we have allegedly become better at multitasking as a result, we've also become much worse at focusing on one thing for extended periods. This makes it harder for us to read a large passage of text for instance, or to work without feeling the need to continuously check Facebook. We're constantly in a state of distraction.

Again, mindfulness is the perfect tonic. Here, you are tasked with focusing on your environment, your thoughts or your feelings for an extended period of time. And, as such, you improve your own focus and mental discipline.

Using the Mindful Approach to Enhance Memory

Using the mindful approach to remember things can be as fun and easy as playing Sudoku and crossword puzzles. Keep in mind that you can't work up to a good memory if you keep thinking you have a bad one — so stop telling yourself that your memory is bad. Use a positive approach and celebrate the times you do remember.

The key to mastering memory is to keep the brain exercised. This stimulates the growth and development of nerve connections which can keep improving the memory. So, basically, the more you exercise your brain, the better your memory becomes.

You can challenge your brain power in many ways using mindful approaches. Besides the normal ways, such as puzzles and memorization, you should get out of your comfort zone and try something new once in a while.

Go back to school to get a degree, learn a new language and new games. Find ways to give your brain the ultimate workout — just as you would if you were trying to exercise your body to become fit.

An Exercise to Help You "Get" Mindfulness: The Body Scan

If you have ever read anything about mindfulness or had any interest in the subject, there's a good chance you might have heard of the body scan technique. For those who haven't heard of this exercise, it's a great introduction to mindfulness and also a great way to strengthen your mind/body connection.

This exercise is also a fantastic way to see just how much you miss by being too inside your own head and forgetting to be present. Read on to give it a try . . .

The Body Scan

The idea of the body scan is to help bring your attention to your own body, your surroundings, and the simple experience of "being." It will take you out of your own head and show you just how much sensory information is coming in at any time.

To begin then, bring your attention to your breath and focus on it with each breath inward and outward.

Continue this for a few minutes and as you do you might notice your mind starts to drift. Don't punish yourself for this, simply make a note of how your mind is working and then bring it back to your experience.

Eventually, you should start to notice other sensations throughout your body. You may notice the feeling of your buttocks on the floor or chair for instance. Perhaps you can feel the light breeze on your skin. Maybe you can feel a slight tension in the muscles of your back.

Gradually expand your awareness to encompass your entire body and then further to encompass the environment around you. Try and listen for sounds in the distance and be aware of how many sounds you can pick up. Don't engage with them, just be aware of them and be constantly aware of your breathing.

Expanding Mindfulness

To extend this to true mindfulness, you're next going to expand your mindfulness even further — this time to encompass your own thoughts so that you're aware of them drifting through your mind like clouds. As with the external sounds earlier, the aim here is not to engage with those thoughts — simply to observe them in a passive manner without assessing or judging them.

If you're interested in trying this exercise but not sure how to go about it yourself, you can find a number of body scan scripts online that will talk you through the process.

The most useful mindfulness tool I found during my path to increase my memory was this quote: ***"Wherever you are, be there."*** In other words, rid yourself of distractions, even if it's just for a moment or two, and be where you are without worrying about where you're going next. Do what you're doing without letting your mind wand to all the other things you need to do in the future.

Mindful Memory Techniques

The mindful approach to memory is now being used by the military to enhance objective attention and general cognition. Studies indicate that even practicing brief, mindful techniques can enhance the working memory and may prevent loss of memory during stress.

Here are 6 tips to use mindful approaches to master memory techniques besides the ones mentioned above:

1. **Learn a new skill.** Anything you'd enjoy and want to learn that's new to you is a great way to improve your memory skills and exercise a larger part of your brain.
2. **Practice better observation.** It's like taking a picture with your brain, but making it as clear as possible. A good example is when we meet people to memorize the face and associate it with the name you're given. Practice saying the name over in your mind and seeing the face at the same time.

3. **Use a variety of senses.** Use as many senses to remember things as you can. The more you stimulate your brain in different areas, the easier it will become to remember and store things for instant recall. For example, writing information on paper by hand stimulates a different part of your brain than memorization from a page. Reading aloud stimulates a different part of your brain than writing. Visual tools, such as flash cards (see the next point), stimulate your brain in yet another way. When you're studying for an exam, practicing varied learning methods can help you remember more.
4. **Flash cards for studying.** You probably remember flash cards in your elementary days of school. It consists of a card of any size with a question on one side and the answer on the other side. Separate the cards you know by heart and those you still need to memorize.
5. **Don't confuse your memory by cramming.** Cramming for a big test or work presentation only stimulates your short-term memory. If you have time, designate study times so your brain can embed the information in your long-term memory. Remember, the short-term memory has capacity limitations, but the long-term memory does not. I've crammed for exams and presentations in the past and felt as though the information "leaked out" of my brain. The truth is, it was never properly embedded into my brain in the first place.
6. **Use items at hand to jog your memory.** If you have to remember to take certain medications on a daily basis, do something like placing your remote control on the refrigerator. When you take the pills, place it back on the coffee table or wherever you normally keep the remote.

The main tip to remembering things is to be able to **focus on it before you move on to something else**. In other words, wherever you are, be there! If something is truly important to remember, study it carefully by avoiding distractions or engaging in other tasks before you have it locked in your memory database.

Main Points about Chapter Three: The Mindful Approach

You can have fun using the mindful approach to improve your memory. Games such as Sudoku and the daily crossword puzzle can increase the nerve cells in your brain and expand its ability to learn. Here are some main things you should know from this chapter:

- **Learn a new skill** — Going back to college or taking online courses can give the brain a good workout.
- **Learn a language** — Much help exists, both online and from CDs and DVDs, to help you learn just about any language you desire. Some studies have indicated that knowing more than one language can help offset the horrors of Alzheimer's Disease.
- **Observe** — Make it a point to intricately observe what you need to remember. It could be a route to a new place or the layout of a school. Take a picture in your mind.
- **Flash cards** — One of the oldest learning methods, flash cards are still good memory builders today.
- **Use things to help you remember** — For example, remember to take your keys with you by putting a chair or other obstacle in front of the door until you have your keys in hand.
- **Focus** — When you really need to remember something, cut out all distractions and attempt to focus solely on what you must remember.

Ultimately mastering your memory means you should constantly exercise your brain in various ways. Mnemonics and the Mindful approach are two ways in which you can enhance your memory by expanding your brain's capability.

Next, we'll learn some memory tricks to give you even more tools to help enhance your memory.

CHAPTER FOUR
Memory Tricks

Memory Tricks

Using certain methods to remember information, faces, numbers, and other things is a tried and true way of tricking your brain into having instant recall when you need it most — studying, traveling, taking a test, giving a presentation, and more.

Memory tricks also involve using your brain and your wits to do things differently. For example, using rhymes which point exactly to what you're trying to remember, using associations such as numbers and words, and mindfulness when can are all ways to trick your mind into remembering certain things.

Franklin Delano Roosevelt was very adept at remembering people's names. He used a trick of imagining the name written across the person's forehead the minute they were introduced. Repeating a name aloud when you're introduced is also used to remember names.

You can keep your brain exercised and vital by playing games, learning new skills, using mnemonic devices and playing tricks on your brain to make an impact. Although it isn't a cure for Alzheimer's disease, keeping your brain active can help to ward off the early symptoms.

Trick Your Brain Techniques

Mastering your memory also includes tricking your brain into remembering vital information. You can trick your brain by thinking outside the box about what helps you remember — is it photographic image taken in your mind? Or, perhaps it's similar to

Roosevelt's method of picturing the name of the person on his or her forehead. Whatever method works to trick your brain can be expanded to include other ways of remembering.

Here are a few tricks you'll want to try:

- **Squeeze a ball.** It's actually been proven that some people can squeeze a stress ball in their dominant hand just before memorizing data. When you're ready to recall the information, squeeze the ball in your non-dominant hand for a few seconds.
- **Speak it.** Say aloud the information you want to remember. For example, if someone is giving you directions, repeat the directions afterward. Saying the information out loud reinforces your memory.
- **Rosemary.** Studies show you can improve your memory recall by smelling the herb, rosemary. You can take rosemary oil or a sprig of rosemary with you and smell it a couple of times per day to get the full effect.
- **Draw a mind map.** Picture a tree in your mind, much like a genealogical family tree, and form the branches with things you must remember. For example, if you have a hectic daily schedule, picture the trunk of the tree as the day and branch off into tasks you must accomplish. This is handy if you're "on the go" and need instant recall.
- **Deep breathing.** The yoga method of deep breathing changes the way your brain operates. If you're going into a lecture or class where it's important for you to remember things, practice deep breathing for a few moments before the event, and you can more easily remember new facts and information.
- **Do something different.** If you need to remember that today is your wedding anniversary, simple wear your watch or your ring on the other hand. It will serve as a quick reminder every time you glance at your hand or check the time.
- **Chewing gum.** Your dentist might not approve, but chewing gum actually stimulates the brain so that you're more focused and can remember more information.

- **Your eyes.** Moving your eyes back and forth for about 30 seconds per day can make your brain operate more effectively. Try it when you wake up in the morning to have more memory recall the rest of the day.

Your brain is a powerful part of your body. No one knows everything we could do if we understood even half of the power it offers. Our brain deteriorates in time, just as our bodies do — so, it's important that you keep exercising your brain (and your body) as you age.

It's fun to test your memory at new skills and at tricking your brain so you remember things important or vital to you. Try all or some of the exercises mentioned in this chapter to keep your memory fresh and your brain active.

Other Ways to Workout Your Memory

Information in your brain is collected, stored, and retrieved by the neural pathways we've mentioned earlier. These pathways are responsible for you being able to solve problems, remember familiar faces, and tasks, without exerting a ton of effort.

An adult has millions of these neural pathways that have developed from infancy. One problem is that you need to continually create new pathways. Changes in your lifestyle, as you age, can often lead to pathways not being developed.

This is because you tend to not exercise as much as you get older. You may not pay as much attention to your diet. Both of these things affect your brain and your memory.

If you stay with your regular habits, you are not challenging your memory. Your brain requires regular stimulation, regardless of your age. It should always be developing and growing pathways.

There are some simple things you can do to stimulate this production of new pathways. Take a new way home from the mall or grocery store. Take up a new exercise or activity such as golf, dancing, yoga, or fishing. Even just going to a museum, an art gallery, or a nature hike in the mountains can stimulate your brain and memory.

Your memory is one of those things you need to use regularly or you run the risk of losing it. If you feel as though you can't remember new things or recall old events, then you may be lacking in the stimulation area.

Any type of activity that uses your hands is a great way to sharpen your memory. Playing a musical instrument is a great option, so is doing needlework or some type of craft. Even putting together a jigsaw puzzle is a great way to get your brain working more effectively.

To really stimulate your memory you should look for activities which are new. This way you have to go through the effort of learning and committing to memory a new skill, with new terms and language. Quite honestly, you want to do something that takes you out of your comfort zone.

Your new activity should be a challenge; puzzles, sports, a new language, challenging crossword puzzles, and learning a new instrument all fit into this category.

In addition, you want your chosen activity to be fun. You should enjoy the challenge and stimulation of learning it. You don't want to dread the time that you spend on it.

While any new activity may be hard at first, the more you continue doing it, the more benefits you will experience. You will have taught yourself something new, added a new skill to your abilities, and you will have increased your neural pathways.

Main Points about Chapter Four: Memory Tricks

Trick your brain by chewing gum? Yes, that's one way that some people employ to memorize information. Performing some varied acts while learning or memorizing information can have a profound effect on the way your brain operates. Here are some of the main things you should have learned in this chapter:

- **Use all your senses** — Using all senses will stimulate your brain in ways that help you remember faces, numbers and volumes of facts. For example, sniffing certain herbs helps to stimulate the brain.
- **Do things differently** — Even wearing your watch on the other arm can help you recall certain information such as birthdays and anniversaries. They're simple tricks that you can make up for your own ways of thinking.

- **Say it aloud** — Sometimes all it takes to remember the name of someone you just met is to repeat his or her name aloud after you're introduced. It reinforces the name so you're more apt to remember it next time.
- **Squeezing a ball** — Stress balls aren't just for relieving stress. You can squeeze one in one hand (and then transfer it to another) to remember all sorts of information.
- **Mind maps are helpful** — Just as you need a map to get you to your destination (if unknown), so can you use a map you formulate in your mind to remember things visually.

It's particularly important to exercise your brain as you age. Just like your body, the brain tends to deteriorate as the aging process takes place. Exercise the brain daily, just as you would your body.

CHAPTER FIVE
Your Lifestyle

Your Memory and Your Lifestyle

All of the previously listed methods in this eBook won't work as well if your lifestyle isn't conducive to boosting your brain power. You know some of the paths to a healthy lifestyle, but those listed in this chapter actually play a huge part in keeping your memory and your body in top condition. This is the area I struggle the most with, and I'm still working on implementing these lifestyle changes to better aid my memory (and my health!).

The brain must be fed and exercised, just as the body, and if you don't exercise, eat unhealthy foods, gain weight, and are generally a couch potato, your brain and your body will suffer the consequences.

This chapter will give you a better understanding about how to better plan your lifestyle and make needed changes so you can live a longer and more fulfilling life. When your mind and body are in sync, you'll be able to accomplish much in your life.

Bad Habits = Bad Memory

Studies are constantly appearing which have us worried about the habits we form in our daily lives. It may have to do with drinking too much, smoking, not getting enough sleep, or too much stress. There's always something we can change to become healthier.

Those bad habits may also be instrumental in hindering your brain health — memory, in particular. Alzheimer's disease is a constant concern among the aging baby boomer population, and it's now sixth in the cause of American deaths. If you have any friends or family members who have suffered from this disease, you know how horrible it is.

Although Alzheimer's is mostly considered a disease of the elderly, bad habits you develop early on can begin a domino effect which can harm your brain and make it easier to become affected by memory diseases.

Here are some habits that can greatly affect your memory and the health of your brain for the worse — some of these will be expounded upon later in this chapter:

- **Poor diet** — A poor diet can take a toll on your brain as well as your body. You may not be able to see the effects on the brain as you can with the body, but the harm is happening is subtle ways such as difficult in focusing, bad memory recall, and poor cognitive functioning.
- **Smoking** — Everyone should know of the harm smoking can cause to the brain, but smoking can also be a factor in decline of memory between the ages of 40 and 50 years old.
- **Lack of sleep** — When you don't get enough sleep at night, you may feel as if you're in a fog during the day. If this condition becomes chronic, you run the risk of damaging the neural pathways of the brain, which may affect memory recall.
- **Lack of exercise** —Your brain can mimic the body when you don't exercise enough. The hippocampus portion of the brain, which is responsible for memory storage, can become sluggish and your cognitive and recall brain functions may be impaired without the proper amount of exercise.
- **Alcohol and drug use** — Some people may have conditions which require prescription drugs for treatment, but overuse of prescription and over-the-counter drugs can greatly impair your ability to remember things. Alcohol consumption may also destroy cells of the brain and make it more difficult to build them back up.

Other reasons to change bad habits are the effects they may have on your body. Heart disease, high cholesterol, cancer, and diabetes may also occur if your bad habits aren't under control.

Tips to Improve Your Memory by the Lifestyle You Lead

As mentioned in the previous section, certain habits and lifestyles can erode your memory and keep you from enjoying the vital and healthy life you could be leading. Smoking, obesity, stress, and other factors can wreak havoc with your brain so that even the techniques mentioned in this eBook won't be of much help.

Just as it "takes a village to raise a child . . ." — it takes caring for your entire body, including your mind — to improve your memory and live an active lifestyle for the rest of your years. Here are some tips to help your memory and stay active:

Get organized — If you're not organized, you risk losing things and becoming stressed and frustrated. You may be perfectly organized at work, but lack that same skill at home. There are all types of ways you can get and stay organized. For example, if you miss deadlines constantly, you can download one of the many applications expressly designed to help you remember important meetings and details. Other organization methods involve objects you might pick up at a container store. Color-coding and other helpful methods can help you stay focused on what's important.

Maintain a Healthy Diet — Dieting isn't only for your body — your brain needs the nutrients you get from eating a diet high in antioxidants that will protect your brain from the free radicals which can inhibit cell production. Foods that contain low glycemic carbohydrates, such as oatmeal, and any food that's comprised of omega-3 fatty acids are good for brain and body. A diet plan such as the Mediterranean Diet concentrates on fruits, vegetables, legumes, fish, and nuts — and low on meat — are recommended. Studies indicate that meat contains omega-6 fatty acids, and that it could contribute to inflammation of the brain — a contributing factor in Alzheimer's disease.

Get plenty of sleep — Sleep is imperative to an effectively functioning brain. Neuroplasticity is the process of brain growth which controls your brain's behavior and how it learns and memorizes. Lack of sleep can eventually erode the neuroplasticity process and impair the memory. For adults — a short afternoon nap has the power to dramatically increase and restore the brain's effectiveness. Even though most adults only need eight hours of sleep per night, you may need more slumbering time if you feel fatigued or sleepy during the day. Both long- and short-term memory may be affect by the amount of sleep you receive. To ensure the sleep you need, go to bed and wake up at the same time and wind down before you go to bed rather than exercising. Also, limit your alcohol use as it interferes with the sleep process. I started taking a 20-minute nap almost every afternoon, and it has really helped revitalize my production in the afternoon and evenings.

Stop multi-tasking — It's been promoted that multi-tasking helps you get through with a job faster, but studies have proven when you're multi-tasking, the brain slows down significantly. If it's important for you to remember how you're doing a task and doing it well, you should be mindful about what you're accomplishing and focus on it completely. That speeds up the brain and helps it preserve memories. Studies show that you should spend at least eight seconds focusing on the task at hand.

Exercise regularly — Exercise is key to enjoying a healthy lifestyle as much as maintaining a healthy diet. When you exercise, nerve cells are stimulated and release neurotrophic factors — an important protein that helps other helpful chemicals to form. Aerobic exercise is especially helpful to improve circulation to the brain and keep from experiencing memory loss that often comes with the aging process. Besides aerobic exercises, engage in strength training, stretching, flexibility and core exercises so that all parts of your body stays healthy. I walk 2-3 miles, at least three or four times per week now, and I feel more energized and alert since I started exercising regularly.

Healthy gut — Maintaining a healthy gut is vital to brain health. The gut produces bacteria which send data to your brain by the vagus nerve – the main cranial nerve that extends from your brain to your gastrointestinal tract's nervous system. Studies indicate that if your gut has abnormal flora, your brain likely has it too and that would prohibit serotonin (a neurotransmitter) which controls mood and depression in your brain. Essentially, your gut health and your brain functions are closely aligned and both must be healthy for ultimate brain health.

Vitamins — Even though you may maintain a healthy diet, you still may not be getting the vitamins and minerals you need for ultimate brain health. If you really want to improve your memory, you should find out if you're deficient in the following vitamins: Vitamin D – Increases nerve growth in your brain that plans and processes new memories. Vitamin D comes from the sun, but you can also take Vitamin D-3 supplements. Vitamin B12 — Slows brain shrinkage, especially in areas most affected by Alzheimer's diseases. Folic acid and vitamins B6 and B12 can lower levels of homocysteine which are associated with brain shrinkage. Omega-3 Fatty Acids — Contain antioxidants which help you brain stay healthy and function properly. Thiamin, Niacin — Foods that contain these vitamins include curry, celery, walnuts, chickpeas, blueberries and healthy oils such as olive and coconut. Fatty fish such as salmon also contain these vital brain vitamins.

Reduce stress — Out of control chronic stress can actually damage the brain and cause remembering to be much harder. You may not be able to reduce all stress from your life, but you can lessen it and learn how to handle it. Relaxation techniques such as yoga and deep breathing can help reduce the harmful effects of stress. Reducing your caffeine intake, massages and spending more time with family and friends can also help.

Laugh — Last, but certainly not least on the list of improving your memory, is to laugh. "Laughter is the best medicine," is really true when it comes to keeping your brain active and healthy.

When you laugh, certain parts of your brain "lights" up like the Fourth of July — especially in the areas of your brain which control your memory. We'll discuss laughter in depth shortly. Pets are also part of training the brain to enjoy life and perk up the memory muscles.

Best Foods for Your Memory

Healthy eating isn't only for your body's fitness — eating the right foods may lower your risk of heart disease, diabetes and heart disease. It may also be a factor in early onset of dementia and Alzheimer's disease.

When you combine certain foods with a healthy and vital lifestyle and brain exercises which can boost memory-saving chemicals, you're taking steps to live a long life and live it on your own terms.

Here are some foods which can make a difference in your brain health and they're great for your body too:

- **Avocado** — Rich in powerful vitamin C and the powerhouse brain-booster of vitamin E, avocado is a food associated with reducing the risk of Alzheimer's disease.
- **Sunflower seeds** — Another food high in vitamin E, sunflower and other seeds can supply 30% of your recommended vitamin E intake in only one ounce.
- **Fruits and Nuts** — Walnuts are a good source of omega-3 fatty acids. Fruits, such as blackberries, blueberries, and cherries, content something called anthocyanin, another memory-boosting element.
- **Fish** — Heart-healthy omega-3 fatty acids (including DHA) are found in tuna, mackerel and salmon. These vitamins are necessary for the brain's neurons are functioning normally.
- **Leafy, dark green vegetables** — Vitamin E and folic acid are found in the food sources of spinach, kale, broccoli and other greens. Eating these healthy foods can lower an amino acid called homocysteine which is found in the blood and may cause death of brain cells. If you aren't a fan of this type of veggie, try eating them in a salad. Or join the green smoothie revolution. Mix up to 2 cups of mixed leafy, dark-greens, add a banana and some berries, mix with water, and you'll have a tasty brain-boosting smoothie to enjoy!
- **Celery** — An often looked-over vegetable to add to your diet is celery. Celery contains luteolin, which helps to reduce inflammation in your brain. This will help reduce the amount of memory loss due to the aging process.
- **Red wine** — Moderate amounts of red wine may prevent the onset of Alzheimer's disease and can greatly improve the bad cholesterol which can lead to heart disease.

- **Berries** — Recent research involving the impact eating berries have on health indicate that acai, blueberries and strawberries may halt the onset of cognitive problems of the memory.
- **Oil-based salad dressing** — These dressings tend to be high in vitamin E and serves as a powerful antioxidant to protect nerve and neuron cells. In many memory-related diseases, neurons begin to deteriorate and eventually cause cognitive problems.
- **Whole grains** — Fiber loaded whole grains should be part of a nutritious diet plan to lower your risk of cognitive impairment and the eventual onset of Alzheimer's disease.

While these foods are important for the continued health of your brain and in preserving your memory, you should combine a good diet with exercise and a healthy lifestyle, free of bad habits and doing everything you can to preserve your brain's health.

Your brain needs the protection and stimulation of good food and exercise the same as the body needs them to stay fit. Pay attention to the foods you eat and you'll reap the benefits of living a long life with a healthy memory in tow.

Best Vitamins and Nutrients for Your Brain Health

Feed your brain the same as you would your body for the ultimate in keeping brain-fit. If you have a deficiency, it can affect your brain in several ways including focus and clarity, mood swings, mental decline, depression and anxiety, dementia, and memory recall.

There are many "supplements" on the market that are promoted to be especially for the brain, but you should know which ones really work. Below are the three essential vitamins and nutrients that are absolutely essential for a healthy brain:

- **Omega-3 Fatty Acids** — Docosahexaenoic acid (DHA) is found in omega-3 fatty acids. DHA is the main building block of the brain and without it, brain problems such as those connected with the nervous system and psychiatric disorders may occur. DHA deficiency may also affect mood swings, depression and anxiety, dementia, Alzheimer's disease, and memory loss. Many of the symptoms of these conditions may be helped with omega-3 fatty acid supplements. Studies have shown that elderly people with high levels of DHA are 50% less likely to suffer from dementia and Alzheimer's as those with lower levels.

- **Vitamin B12** — If you find yourself having difficult recalling information and feel that you're in a fog most of the time, you may be deficient in a B-complex vitamin. Studies show there's a connection between Vitamin B12 deficiency and the two most feared conditions of the elderly — dementia and Alzheimer's disease. Since people may have a difficult time absorbing Vitamin B12 as they age, a vitamin supplement may be in order. Be sure and check your B-level vitamins during your yearly checkup.
- **Vitamin D** — This vitamin is close to DHA in importance to the brain's health and memory recall. Vitamin D can get rid of depression and anxiety, help you focus, and help you be better able to solve problems. Besides having a profound effect on your memory, Vitamin D can also protect against such diseases as diabetes, heart disease, and cancer. Your bone density can also be affected by a deficiency of this vitamin and may prevent osteoporosis, which is a leading cause of hip fractures.

Other vitamins which are also important to brain health include antioxidants, which can help rid your body of free radicals that can harm the neural pathways in the brain.

"Smart drugs" have become popular brain boosters and are only available by prescription, but you should speak to your physician before deciding to go this route.

You can enhance your brain power and memory recall by ensuring your body is getting the proper vitamins and nutrients. If not, supplements can make a difference.

Caffeine and Your Memory

Most of the time you associate drinking caffeine as something which is bad for you. When it comes to your memory, though, this may be another ball game altogether.

A recent study was conducted by the John Hopkins University in Baltimore, Maryland. This study determined that caffeine can improve certain memories for up to a day after the memory has been formed.

This seems to help solidify the reasoning behind students drinking energy drinks and filling up on coffee and tea right before an exam. A shot of caffeine can boost your memory. (But, like anything else, don't overdo it, or you'll suffer from the negative side-effects.)

Previously any findings on the benefits of caffeine had been dismissed. So why now are people agreeing that caffeine can indeed help?

Your actual state of mind could determine just how well a boost of caffeine can improve your memory. When you register memories from reading, it seems that the more eager you are the more information you will retain.

This is a different concept to seeing how your natural alertness increases due to drinking coffee or tea. In an attempt to differentiate from being eager and willing, to seeing just how much more alert a person became, an alternative approach was necessary.

In the new study, 73 volunteers were asked to look at images of objects, for example, plants, a horse, a basket, or a musical instrument. Once the group had looked at the objects half were given caffeine, the equivalent to about two cups of strong espresso. The remaining volunteers were give a placebo.

The doctors took saliva samples on a 1, 3, and 24 hour basis and measured the participants caffeine levels.

The next day everyone was asked to look at a new set of images. Now, some of these images were the same, some were very similar, and others were brand new. The goal of the doctors was to see who could identify the changes that had been made.

The study showed that those volunteers who had the caffeine found it easier to identify similar pictures. They were much more alert and picked out the similar images more easily. The group who had taken the placebo could tell which images were old and which were new. But they had a harder time when it came to the similar images.

This research test was conducted differently to a standard recognition memory test. Viewing the images uses a part of your brain that distinguishes between patterns called the hippocampus. To do this effectively you need to have good short- and long-term memory.

This type of test is much more difficult and uses a separation process in your memory. This is the process that is enhanced by caffeine and means that drinking coffee may not be as bad for you as was once thought.

The Benefits of Sleep

Everyone recognizes the importance of sleep. When you miss sleep, you feel tired and have no energy, plus your moods and general well-being change.

A ton of research has gone into understanding the benefits of sleep. Sleep has been shown to help improve immune function, your metabolism, your memory, as well as your ability to learn. Sleep is required so that your body can run and perform at optimal levels.

Sleep has been shown to help boost learning and memory function. There are two main benefits connected with this and sleep. The first one is quite simple — a person who is deprived of sleep just cannot focus properly, so they will not learn effectively. The second benefit is that after learning something new, your memory consolidates this information while sleeping. So studying just before going to bed is a good thing.

Getting adequate sleep has also been linked with living longer. Research shows that people who slept under 5 hours per night were more likely to die early. This does not mean that you want to oversleep either, as too much sleep is also connected with a shorter life span.

Your health can also be affected by the quality of your sleep. People who sleep less than 6 hours a day often suffer with health issues such as arthritis, diabetes, stroke, and heart disease.

This has been linked to them having more inflammatory protein levels in their blood. When these issues are treated and more sleep is achieved, the protein levels have been shown to decline.

Your creativity levels, athleticism and school grades can all improve by sleeping more. It was discovered that many children with **ADHD** were actually sleep deprived. It is recommended that young children get more than 8 hours of sleep per night.

If you are trying to lose weight, sleep has additional benefits. Dieters who sleep more find that they can lose weight more quickly. This is because your metabolism and sleep are controlled by the same areas of your brain. If losing weight is your goal, then try and get a good night's rest every night.

As you can see, sleep really does have a major impact not just on your memory, but on your life. If you are having difficulty sleeping then look for ways to improve this.

Stress Can Sabotage Your Memory

You may know about how stress can affect your body — making it difficult to sleep so you're groggy during the day, depression, anxiety, and inability to focus on work and other tasks. Your memory can also be highly affected by chronic or extreme stress.

The memory works by processing information we acquire through the pathways of the brain. We can retain and recall experiences and things we've learned in the past through the neural pathways we've talked about.

Short-term memory (working memory) is what we notice or think of first when we're reading or memorizing something. Then, it's processed into the long-term memory — if conditions are healthy in your brain. Here's a recap of the three stages that information goes through before it's processed into the long-term memory:

1. Encoding — Encoding happens when you listen or observe something. You must move on to the next two stages for it to stay in your memory.
2. **Consolidation** — Much like you would burn a CD, consolidated information becomes burned into your memory so you can move on to the next stage.

3. **Retrieval** — The part of your brain which allows you to recall the information you encoded and consolidated.

Stress may interfere with either or all of these memory processing stages in the following ways:

- **Interference** — Stress can interfere with any of the above processes by distracting what you're trying to remember. For example, if you've just memorized some important information and then experience a stressful situation, you're not likely to remember the data you were trying to process.
- **Not finishing the process** — If you don't complete all three of the stages to process memories, you probably didn't encode it in the first place. For example, if you forget an important business meeting, you likely just heard the date and time, but didn't write it down or think of it in ways to remember it and store it in your long-term memory.
- **Stress hormones** — Stress can create stress hormones that may prevent passage of memories through the neural pathways. These hormones interfere with the chemical balance of your brain and can greatly reduce your recall ability.

A certain amount of stress can actually be good for you – especially when it's involved with emotions. You can probably remember some traumatic event that happened in your life because it was an emotional experience and your brain recorded every detail.

We're born with a certain amount of this ingrained emotional memory ability because of the "fight or flight" response that is embedded into all human beings. Think about the stress in your own life and how it may be affecting your memory recall.

Why Laughter Really Is the Best Medicine

A recent study indicates that laughter can boost your memory and also help your overall demeanor. Magnetic resonance shows that when you laugh, your brain lights up just as it would when exercised by a brain-teaser. Exercise is good for your brain and can instantly improve your mood, mask pain, and even make for better relationships.

Many consider humor and laughter a silly diversion, but in fact, the neuropsychological benefits are astounding. When you hear the end of a joke or struggle to get a punchline in an anecdote, your brain gets a huge workout.

When you laugh, a chemical reaction takes place in your brain which helps your entire makeup. Here are a few benefits of laughter:

- **Boosts immunity** — Your immune system can greatly benefit from laugher, which can be suppressed from stress and pain.
- **Reduces stress and pain** — The chemical reaction from laughter is directly connected to the nucleus accumbens in the brain. This area of the brain releases dopamine, which is a natural opiate.
- **Bonding with others** — Developing relationships is an important part of keeping a healthy brain. Laughter can repel anger. Laughter promotes reconciliation and is said to be one of the most desired traits in a life partner.

Studies performed with groups watching a funny movie indicated more improvement in memory recall, cognitive functions, and the ability to learn compared with other groups who didn't watch the movie.

Diabetics, especially, benefited from laughter because it cuts down on the harmful hormone of cortisol and boosted memory scores. Cortisol may also decrease the hippocampal neurons, which make up the memory portion of the brain. It increases the flow of blood and boosts your mood.

The increase of dopamine and endorphins in the brain when you laugh can provide pleasure and sense of accomplishment. Laughter also promotes neurochemical brain changes which increase the memory enhancement — gamma wave band frequency.

Try and add some elements of laughter to your life each day and use humor to deflect negative thoughts from entering your mind.

Before you settle down to sleep at night, watch a funny show or ready a funny book to get your evening of rest off to a good start.

Recent studies have been so positive in the use of laughter to improve memory and overall health of the elderly that humor may be incorporated in wellness programs designed for senior citizens.

All of your worries may not simply melt away with adding more laughter in your life, but try it for a while. It's definitely true that "laughter may improve memory and quality of life."

Main Points of Chapter Five: Your Lifestyle

If your lifestyle is in the ditch, your memory will be also. You've got to match your lifestyle with how you want your brain to work. That means eating a healthy diet, exercise (both body and brain) and keeping stress at bay. The main points of this chapter are:

- **Organize your life** so that it's uncluttered — and your brain will be also.
- **Sleep** is imperative to keep your brain active. Make sure you get plenty of uninterrupted sleep each night and take cat naps during the day, if needed.
- **Don't multi-task.** When you multi-task, your focusing abilities are off. Your memory is better served when performing one task at a time.
- **Eat healthy.** Your brain needs the proper nutrients as much as your body, so it's important to eat healthy if you want to maintain brain health throughout life.
- **Keep your gut (digestive tract) healthy.** The gut produces bacteria that's necessary to keep the brain humming.
- **Exercise your brain and your body**. Cardio is necessary to provide oxygen to the brain and keep the memory far into the aging process.
- **Check your vitamins.** Vitamin D, B and Omega-3 fatty acids are essential to good brain health.
- **Laugh.** You should also laugh often. Laughter stimulates the brain as much as any of the above techniques. It's a part of life that you should cultivate.

CHAPTER SIX
Mastering Memory

Mastering Memory — One Step at a Time

In this chapter we are going to review some of the tips, ideas, and strategies suggested in the previous chapters. Then we are going to give you a chance to develop an action plan so that you can put some (or all) of the suggested ideas into action in your own life.

This is your opportunity to commit to develop a strong memory now and for years to come! So let's have some fun with it. Below you'll find some Action Guides to help you boost that memory. You can refer to these guides or create your own, using the memory-boosting tactics you found most helpful.

Mnemonic Devices Action Guide

Mnemonic Devices	Action Item
Association	Create an association to help you remember something important in your life right now. For example if you need to remember that Franklin Roosevelt was president during World War II, you could associate his last name with an image of roses (for Roose) and velvet (velt). Velvet roses are a good image for the name.
Rhymes	Create a rhyme to help you remember something important in your life right now. For example, "Columbus sailed the ocean blue in fourteen- hundred ninety-two."
Chunking	Try memorizing your driver's license number by chunking it into blocks of 3

Acronyms	**Create an acronym to help you remember something important in your life right now.** For example, H-O-M-E-S, for remembering the Great Lakes – Huron, Ontario, Michigan, Erie and Superior
Acrostics	**Use an acrostic approach to help you remember something important in your life right now.** For example, to remember the five elements in the chemistry periodic table (Hydrogen, Helium, Lithium, Beryllium, Boron), you might make up the following sentence: "His Heavy Load Breaks Backs."
Loci	**Use the loci approach to help you remember something important in your life right now.** For example, arrange your grocery list by aisles and picture going down each one in order of your list.
Stacking	**Use the stacking method to help you remember something important in your life right now.** For example, if you need to remember several items at the pet store (treats, food, sweater, leash and shampoo), you could picture a tall stack of dog food wrapped in a warm doggie sweater with treat bags sticking out of the neck. Put the leash around the neck of the sweater, your dog on top of the stack (with its fur bubbly with shampoo).

Mindful Approach Action Guide

Mindful Approach	Action Item
Learn a New Skill	Choose a new skill to learn as part of your efforts to improve your memory long term.
Practice Better Observation	Practice remembering a new person you meet by seeing and repeating their name with their face.
Use a Variety of Senses	Use multiple senses to help

	you remember something important in your life right now.
	For example, write down an important piece of information and repeat it out loud as you write it.
Flash Cards for Studying	Use flash cards to help you remember something important in your life right now.
	For example, you could use flash cards to help you remember how to perform new tasks at work.
Use Items at Hand to Jog Memory	Use an item at hand to help you remember something important in your life right now.
	For example, if you have to remember to take certain medications on a daily basis, do something like placing your remote control on the refrigerator.

Memory Tricks Action Guide

Memory Tricks	Action Item
Squeeze a Ball	Try the squeezing a ball technique to help you remember something important in your life right now.
	For example, squeeze a ball in your dominant hand while memorizing your doctor's phone number. Later, squeeze the ball with your other hand while trying to recall the number.
Speak It	**Try speaking aloud to help**

	you remember something important in your life right now.
	For example, if someone is giving you directions, repeat the directions afterwards. Saying the information out loud reinforces your memory.
Rosemary	**Go purchase some rosemary from the whole foods store and try smelling it a few times a day for the next 2 weeks. Pay attention for any improvements with your memory.**
Draw a Mind Map	**Go purchase some rosemary from the whole foods store and try smelling it a few times a day for the next 2 weeks. Pay attention for any improvements with your memory.**
Deep Breathing	**Try deep breathing to help you remember something important in your life right now.** For example, if you are about to study or learn something new, try taking a series of deep breaths first.
Do Something Different	**Try doing something different to help you remember something important in your life right now.** For example, if you need to remember that today is your wedding anniversary, simple wear your watch or your ring on the other hand. It will serve as a quick reminder every time you glance at

	your hand or check the time.
Your Eyes	**Starting today try the method of moving your eyes back and forth for 30 seconds as a way to stimulate your brain. Repeat for a few weeks and observe the results.**

These action items will give you a great starting point for not only understanding how to improve your memory, but actually putting the memory exercises into practice.

Before we send you on your way, there is one additional area to cover that is vital to understanding memory and memory performance.

Serious Problems Which May Affect Your Memory

The techniques discussed in this eBook can help train your brain to be at its healthiest and most active — helping you preserve your memory skills. Your brain is a vibrant organ and is constantly changing — sometimes for the worse.

The brain's central memory area — the hippocampus — is there to regenerate the brain's cells throughout your life. Your brain can keep regenerating far into your later years if you know and practice the techniques designed to keep it active.

When you go about your daily activities, your brain is "recharged" with every new and healthy thing you accomplish and learn. If you lack sleep on a daily basis your brain can be affected in a negative manner and if you eat an unhealthy diet or never exercise, you can run the risk of interfering with your ability to remember.

But, a healthy lifestyle and some stimulation to the brain in the form of mnemonics and mindful approaches can encourage your brain to produce new neurons. This process is called neuroplasticity or neurogenesis and is the most powerful way to regenerate your brain for years to come.

There are some factors that can affect your memory and which you need to control:

- **Thyroid gland** — The thyroid doesn't directly affect your brain, but if you suffer from hyperthyroidism or hypothyroidism, you can have difficulty with focusing and remembering things. Addressing the problem with your health care provider can help to solve the problem.
- **Frequent infections** — Those who are more prone to viruses or infections and who are more apt to succumb to germs score lower on cognitive tests than those with a lower risk factor. Damage to blood vessels may be the cause for this anomaly.
- **Menopause** — The ravages of menopause can include factors such as how well your sleep and loss of memory. Although this is only a temporary problem, there are some solutions you can try to alleviate the symptoms. Drinking green tea and reducing stress are just a couple of ways to reduce the negative effects of menopause.
- **Anxiety/Depression** — Stress hormones are increased by anxiety and depression. When this happens, your brain loses the ability to connect brain cells (synapses). When this occurs, you may have less ability to keep and retrieve memories.
- **Medications** — Certain medications can interfere with your brain and memory functions. Anxiety medications, in particular, can obstruct the ability of the brain to transition short-term memories into long-term memories. Drugs such as Xanax, Ativan, and Valium can severely limit the brain's functioning powers. Some over-the-counter medications, such as Benadryl, can also affect memory.

We live in a society where cognitive functions are highly regarded and even the least little fear that we're "losing it" is cause for alarm. Misplacing your keys or not having instant recall of someone's name is no longer considered being "absent-minded," but a symptom of something much more threatening.

Greater fear about memory loss has led to much more public awareness of dementia, Alzheimer's disease, and a growing concern about how to keep our brains functioning at their top levels far into old age.

This eBook is designed to help you overcome your fear of losing your memory and put you in control of your brain and how it operates.

Hopefully, you'll gain a new knowledge and make a plan about what you're going to do to keep your brain functioning at its ultimate height. The techniques contained in this guide should put you at ease about your memory and put you on the right path of preserving it — for a lifetime.

CHAPTER SEVEN

Bonus Item — Mastering Memory Checklist

Mastering Memory

Using Mnemonic Devices

- ☐ Association is a form of mnemonic exercise that involves associating factual information with an image or of breaking up long numbers in a shorter format to remember more easily.
- ☐ Rhymes can help you recall facts and information. "Columbus sailed in ocean blue in fourteen-hundred ninety-two." Students of all ages find this method easy when trying to memorize volumes of information.
- ☐ Chunking is also a fun and easy mnemonic device. You'll group things (anything) together to form something that's easy to remember. For example, "Detergent, Olive oil and Green beans" forms the word, "DOG," which you can then break out into the items when needed.
- ☐ Acronyms are best for remember a great deal of information for instant recall. Many students recall the Great Lakes for a test by remembering the word, H-O-M-E-S, which translates to Huron, Ontario, Michigan, Erie and Superior.
- ☐ Acrostics are great ways to remember things that don't make sense otherwise. For example make a sentence out of CABS by thinking "Chronic Asthma Brings Sickness."
- ☐ Loci has been used since the ancient days of Greece and involves memorizing things or people on a path that you're

familiar with. As you walk down the route or path, visualize the things you want to remember appearing along the way.
- ☐ Stacking is another fun way of using visualization to remember things. You can use your vivid imagination to build a picture of things on a list you must remember.

The Mindful Approach

- ☐ Learn a new skill – Going back to college or taking college courses can give the brain a good workout.
- ☐ Learn a language – Much help exists, both online and from CDs and DVDs to help you learn just about any language you desire.
- ☐ Observe – Make it a point to intricately observe what you need to remember. It could be a route to a new place or the layout of a school. Take a picture in your mind.
- ☐ Flash cards – One of the oldest learning methods, flash cards are still good memory builders today.
- ☐ Use things to help you remember – For example, remember to take your keys with you by putting a chair or other obstacle in front of the door until you have your keys in hand.
- ☐ Focus – When you really need to remember something, cut out all distractions and attempt to focus solely on what you must remember.

Memory Tricks

- ☐ Use all your senses – Using all senses will stimulate your brain in ways that help you remember faces, numbers and volumes of facts. For example, sniffing certain herbs helps to stimulate the brain.
- ☐ Do things differently – Even wearing your watch on the other arm can help you recall certain information such as birthdays and anniversaries. They're simple tricks that you can make up for your own ways of thinking.
- ☐ Say it aloud – Sometimes all it takes to remember the name of someone you just met is to repeat his or her name aloud

after you're introduced. It reinforces the name so you're more apt to remember it next time.
- ☐ Squeezing a ball – Stress balls aren't just for relieving stress. You can squeeze one in one hand (and then transfer it to another) to remember all sorts of information.
- ☐ Mind maps are helpful – Just as you need a map to get you to your destination (if unknown), so can you use a map you formulate in your mind to remember things visually.

Your Lifestyle

- ☐ Organize your life so that it's uncluttered – and your brain will be also.
- ☐ Sleep is imperative to keep your brain active. Make sure you get plenty of uninterrupted sleep each night and take cat naps during the day, if needed.
- ☐ Don't multi-task. When you multi-task, your focusing abilities are off. Your memory is better served when performing one task at a time.
- ☐ Eat healthy. Your brain needs the proper nutrients as much as your body, so it's important to eat healthy if you want to maintain brain health throughout life.
- ☐ Keep your gut (digestive tract) healthy. The gut produces bacteria that's necessary to keep the brain humming.
- ☐ Exercise your brain and your body. Cardio is necessary to provide oxygen to the brain and keep the memory far into the aging process.
- ☐ Check your vitamins. Vitamin D, B and Omega-3 fatty acids are essential to good brain health.

ABOUT THE AUTHOR

Linda Fulkerson is a blog coach, marketing consultant, and owner of a digital services company. She is the author of several marketing and self-help books. Linda lives with her husband on a hobby farm in central Arkansas. Her hobbies include traveling and photography.

To learn more about Linda or to access free training on marketing and writing, visit her website at www.LindaFulkerson.com.